Passing Glances

AF632829

Elise Anne Cassista

BookLeaf Publishing

Passing Glances © 2023 Elise Anne Cassista

All rights reserved.

No part of this publication may be reproduced, stored in a retrieval system, or transmitted, in any form or by any means, electronic, mechanical, photocopying, recording or otherwise, without the prior written permission of the presenters.

Elise Anne Cassista asserts the moral right to be identified as author of this work.

Presentation by *BookLeaf Publishing*

Web: www.bookleafpub.com

E-mail: info@bookleafpub.com

ISBN: 9789357213172

First edition 2023

to be a poet is to crack open
to fissure from the former fontanelle
to split sutures open to the soul

fuck the taboo
this is me
unfiltered and unapologetic
maybe a little apologetic
from societal pressure and people pleasing
tendencies
but unapologetically oriented

and purposefully apologetic to my parents
i'm sorry this anthology has sex in it
you can cover your eyes and yell "lalala"

i'm weird
for that i carry no apology

i hurt
for that i carry no apology

i'm struggling
for that i carry no apology

i have eternal hope
for that i carry no apology

"fracture"

hope for contentment
good enough does enough good
contentment for hope

“symmetry”

I feel thin, sort of stretched,
like avocado scraped over
too much toast.

“Millennial JRR Tolkien”

chased by a tiger
enormous paws denting earthen paths
silent yet heard deep within my gut
teeth ready to sink
deep
piercing through muscle
surrounding my spine

shake shake shake

the tiger fades

shake shake shake

movement from top to toe, limbs flail

the tiger recedes into the shadows
melts into the mist
it isn't corporeal anyway

"Anxiety"

Laugh react. Like react. Love react.
Comment: gif with the cute baby
Post: proud of how far i've come

Like react. Like react. Laugh react.
Comment: i'm dead!

Love react.
Comment: omigosh yay!

Like react. Like react. Laugh react.
Like react. Like react.

numb.

"Doomscrolling"

unload the dishwasher
load of laundry
clean out the junk drawer
clean out the storage closet
donate excess possessions
meditate 20 minutes daily
wake at 4am with joy
find work-life balance
discover irrefutable proof of unicorns

“sometimes the difficulty feels the same”

my tongue-tied soul
tries to creep out

through pen strokes
hip gyrations
flickers of candlelight

reedy recitations

thwarted again by the constraints of a body

"i need to get out of my own way"

Without judgment how free
How libertine might we be
Nineteenth century upright queens
Drank laudanum without question
No war on humans coping
From too much burden
Shoulders broken under the weight
Yoked to a life they don’t want
Failed by absolutes

“Question Everything”

november14
set Specific Measurable Achievable Relevant
Time-bound goals
career:
-
january1
Vision Board Workshop Notes:
*6 unmutes phone participants

march18
brightly colored drawing of a hairy vulva

may23
I am really afraid of vaginas. mine a little, others' a lot.

june8
it's okay to love conditionally

october4
to do:
-actually fucking make the call
-stew about the call for hours first

november9
past puts here & now in context

"you've read my diary"

i am not meant to be sober
to make steady, staid choices
i too would have chosen a stranger
not steady as a drum
handsome, good provider Koku'um
the mouse at least got that right

if only I could see the world
corner to corner
stitch to stitch
ocean to ocean
pen stroke to pen stroke

art is my purpose
a purpose i cannot reach
yet reaches to me

"Curiosity is my Muse"

fat useless lazy disgusting
unworthy needy ugly unloveable
stupid selfish incapable whore

I was taught to ignore what they said.

"Inner Monologue"

if i were meant to seize the day
i'd have a net
to catch the butterfly
without crushing it between clumsy fingers

"clumsy diem"

They don’t leave
They stay behind
    wandering aimlessly through a world in which
                                                    they no longer belong

They reach
(and claw)
They whisper
(and scream)
                claiming connection that isn’t because it
                                                            provides comfort

yet Beloved are no longer

They reach
(and claw)
They whisper
(and scream)
keeping them from a world they no longer know.

“through a veil”

Candlelight warmed tobacco stains
Tattoos of a former resident
Hover above me
Water beating down my back
I'm never alone

Shadows of souls lasso me
Their life, their memories are ours
We share tears
The light flickers
I am never alone

"Ghosts of Apartment Present"

buoyant and weightless
lunar apogee unseen over head
words become brush strokes
eternity in an instant
i've seen the eclipsing eye of the universe and it
saw me

"float"

out of My skin

husk

remnant

doppelganger

can You tell

is it Me

am I gone

if I find Myself
maybe I'll be whole

"when I find Myself
I'll be whole"

it was 10 years since
listening to music sober
used it to keep you contained
my genie, only granting pain

pain filtered through intoxication
told our story yet hid
tear tracks on your face
scars on your arm
i remember the blood before they were scars
set of your jaw
the way your hair was tousled

recollection not necessary
particularly not how i sent you packing
my brain said no
i'll never forgive myself

it was 10 years awhile ago
i've learned to listen to music sober
appreciate the swells
of love guilt anger joy
between each note
or cried lyric

you're still there
i can bear our story now

"it was still the right choice"

I am empowered to be a diplomat
and not to acquiesce
be a broken record.

change my perspective

the situation is not my fault
yet staying in it is

"Worthy of Boundaries"

one day, my lucky
red pen which writes in black ink
will run dry, not yet

“haiku for a great pen”

If only I were a witch
then my burning would make sense

ashes to ashes
dust to dust
passed to past
combustion to Someone

"Thompson's Motif Index: Motif B32"

proud sheep
seeking herding dog
to guide and protect

proud shepherd
sees the sheep
for the herding dog she really is

"you are what you seek"

www.ingramcontent.com/pod-product-compliance
Lightning Source LLC
Chambersburg PA
CBHW062112140826
49812CB00058B/1314
* 9 7 8 9 3 5 7 2 1 3 1 7 2 *